TALKING WITH ARTISTS

✢ ✢ ✢

VOLUME THREE

TALKING WITH ARTISTS

❖ ❖ ❖

VOLUME THREE

CONVERSATIONS WITH

PETER CATALANOTTO • RAÚL COLÓN
LISA DESIMINI • JANE DYER
KEVIN HAWKES • G. BRIAN KARAS
BETSY LEWIN • TED LEWIN
KEIKO NARAHASHI • ELISE PRIMAVERA
ANNA RICH • PETER SÍS
PAUL O. ZELINSKY

COMPILED AND EDITED BY

PAT CUMMINGS

CLARION BOOKS • NEW YORK

CLARION BOOKS
a Houghton Mifflin Company imprint
215 Park Avenue South, New York, NY 10003

The text of this book is set in 14-point Garamond #3
Printed in Singapore.

Library of Congress Cataloging-in-Publication Data

Talking with artists.
p.   cm.
Includes bibliographical references.
Summary: Distinguished picture book artists talk about their early art experiences,
answer questions most frequently asked by children, and offer encouragement to aspiring artists.
ISBN: 0-395-89132-9
1. Illustrators—United States—Biography—Juvenile Literature.
[1. Illustrators. 2. Artists.]
I. Cummings, Pat.
NC975.T34   1991
741.6'42'092273   [B]   91-9982
ISBN 0-02-724245-5 (v. 1)
ISBN 0-689-80310-9 (v. 2)

TWP   10 9 8 7 6 5 4 3 2

For Dorothy Briley

❖   ❖   ❖

•••••• CONTENTS ••••••

Dear Reader,

I was working with a group of students who were illustrating their own stories and I noticed that one boy named Sergio would only draw tiny, tiny pictures and only in black and white. It was hard to tell what they were. He said that was how he liked to draw.

But the difference between drawing for yourself and illustrating something is that your illustration is going to be seen by others. In fact, the word *illustrate* comes from a Latin word that means *to throw light on something*. So an illustration has to communicate something. The group and I finally convinced Sergio that if he drew larger, his picture might work better for the story.

The next time we met, he brought in a fantastic, much larger drawing of a time-travel machine complete with all kinds of mechanical knobs and buttons and special features. It was incredible. The details he incorporated almost made you believe that the machine might really work. It also made a great illustration for his story.

All thirteen of the artists in this volume are very talented at communicating. They all work in different styles but their work really seems to take you right into the mood of the story they are illustrating. Some of their stories are funny, some are mysterious, and some may make you think of something similar that happened to you. But all of the artists read their stories and thought about how to communicate in pictures what the story meant to them.

In this third volume, everyone answers the same questions as in the first two books. Also, because the secret techniques in volume 2 were so helpful, I asked this new group of illustrators if they would share some drawing tips. And this time, we get a peek at some of their pets. I'm not sure, but I think a few of these dogs and cats may even show up in some of their books.

These artists use every material from the softest pastels to pixels in a computer, and with great results. Experimenting is probably the best thing you can do to improve your drawing and to keep it fun.

Next time I see Sergio, I'm going to show him the work done by the artists in this book. And maybe I can convince him to try a little color.

—Pat Cummings

BIRTHDAY: March 21, 1959
Peter Catalanotto

MY STORY

When I was in second grade I believed I would grow up and work as an artist. I thought that meant I would move to New York City, spend my entire life drawing and painting, slowly starve to death, and, after I was dead, people would start buying my paintings. The scary part is, this appealed to me as an eight-year-old. It seemed a noble and romantic life. I will admit, however, when I learned I could sell my art while I was still alive, I liked that better.

I grew up on Long Island. I was the second of five children. My whole family loved to draw. There was a wall in the basement my parents let us draw on. We'd fill the entire wall with television characters and comic-book heroes. My favorites were the Fantastic Four, the X-Men, and Spider-Man. When there was no more space to draw, my mom or dad would paint the wall white and we'd start anew.

One of the best things I remember about drawing as a child was finding a great pencil, one with a point that is hard enough to make crisp outlines yet soft enough for shading. A great pencil made me feel I could draw anything. I'd hide it from my brothers and sisters in my sock drawer at night. I'd use it until it was so small it would hurt my palm when I drew with it. Great pencils were hard to find.

I was a very shy child and drawing helped me meet kids and make friends in school. I loved it when teachers asked me to decorate their bulletin boards. I also liked drawing for my classmates but sometimes I had to draw the same picture twenty-five times.

I loved to draw animals when I was in elementary school. My favorite animal to draw was my dog, a German shepard named King. When I grew up, the first book that I wrote and illustrated, *Dylan's Day Out,* was inspired by my dog, Beau. Animals are still my favorite things to draw. When I illustrate books by other authors I like to add extra animals to the story.

When I visit elementary schools I love to look at watercolor pictures by the students. A lot of kids tell me they wish they could draw and paint like I do. I wish I could draw and paint like them, so free, powerful, and expressive.

The more you practice with watercolor paints the more control you'll have over what happens in your painting. But too much control isn't good because your paintings might look stiff. Many children think the more a painting looks like a photograph the better it is as a painting, and students get upset and discouraged because they can't make that happen. Painting like photographs is just one way of painting.

I think if you want something to look like a photograph you should use a camera. Paintings are supposed to look like paintings. And there are many different ways to paint. So if your colors always mix into each other or your paints constantly drip, you probably need to use less water and more patience. But the next time something happens in your picture that you didn't plan, stop and take a good look at it. You might like it and try it in your next picture.

Painting should be fun. Try new things. Mistakes and problems are part of the creative process and will help you develop your own style. If your pictures look different than your classmate's—that's good! It would be fiercely dull if we all painted the same way. Be an artist!

"Don't let anyone make you feel that you can't draw. Remember, everyone draws differently!"
—*Peter Catalanotto*

King and I.
Age 5. Pencil, 9 x 6".

Where do you get your ideas?

My ideas start with things that really happen to me and then I add what I wish would happen. Imagining "What if . . . ?" is a wonderful way to get ideas.

When I go to bed at night, "What if" the Sandman, Jack Frost, the Tooth Fairy, and Santa Claus all show up in my room?!

When I go shopping, "What if" I ask for a can of stew, but I'm misunderstood and I get a kangaroo?!

Artists have the power to make anything happen in their pictures and stories.

What is a normal day like for you?

I start each day with fifty "Hurry up or you'll miss the bus"es to my daughter. After Chelsea's on the bus I go for a walk. Walking helps me plan my day. Also, since I'll be sitting for hours painting, it's important for me to exercise.

If I'm writing a book I like to write in the morning. Writing always makes me hungry, so I eat lunch at 11 A.M. After lunch I start painting. At 3:30 I meet Chelsea at the bus stop and we do whatever she wants: play games, paint, draw on the driveway, or ride bicycles. After supper I help her with her homework. Then we read. I read to her. She reads to me. Then we read our own books for a while. When Chelsea's asleep I go back to work in my studio.

I love painting at night. There are less distractions and I feel I have more energy. But sometimes I stay up too late and after my morning walk I have to take a nap!

Where do you work?

My studio is above the garage. I can go to work in pajamas! The best part of working at home is watching Chelsea grow up. I was there for her first word, "Dada," and her first steps. The only bad part is that when I'm home I feel I should be working. Sometimes I can't relax in my own house! My wife, Jo-Ann, a photographer, also works at home. We wonder when Chelsea's going to say, "Hey! How come I'm the only one who has to leave the house every morning!"

Do you have any children? Any pets?

Chelsea's a smart, funny, and passionate second-grader. She loves to draw, write, read, swim, sing, and play the piano. When she grows up she wants to get a job protecting wolves. She's everything I want in a child!

We have a German shepherd named ChaCha.

What do you enjoy drawing the most?

I like drawing natural things like animals, people, clouds, and trees, and not hard boxy things like cars, buildings, and boxes.

I especially love to paint light and shadow. I put lots of colors in shadows. As a kid I made all shadows black. Shadows are hardly ever black, only when the surface they're on is black. There are usually lots of wonderful muted colors in shadows.

Do you ever put people you know in your pictures?

I always do. My wife and daughter, my dog, my house, and myself are in *The Painter*. Sometimes I paint people the way they really look, but sometimes I have to change them so they look like the characters I need in my books.

In *An Angel for Solomon Singer* I painted my thirty-two-year-old brother as a sixty-three-year-old man. Nobody likes it when I make them look older or heavier.

Chelsea and ChaCha

What do you use to make your pictures?

The paintings in my books are watercolors on illustration board. I like watercolors because there are different ways to use them. Transparent, to show dreams, motion, and time passing, or I can paint thicker to show solid objects.

When I first started using watercolors it was frustrating, but after years of practicing I've learned how to create many effects with them.

The Painter.
1995. Watercolor,
17½ x 10½".
Published by
Orchard Books.

How did you get to do your first book?

In 1987, after I painted a couple of book covers for an editor named Richard Jackson, he asked me to paint a picture book. The first book I tried didn't work out. Even though Jackson liked my sketches, he didn't think they were right for the book. I was afraid I had messed up. But three weeks later he gave me another story and *All I See* became my first picture book in 1988.

Raúl Colón

BIRTHDAY: December 17, 1952
Raúl Colón

MY STORY

For as long as I can remember I knew I wanted to draw. Mom usually had paper lying around so I always picked up a pencil or an art pen and drew. One of my first pictures was of a huge trailer truck. I also read a lot of comic books and started drawing from them. I had chronic asthma as a child so I missed a lot of school. I spent hours just watching TV and drawing. I practically forced my sister to give me her notebooks from school and I would fill them up. My father helped me learn how to draw faces by first making a grid on paper and a grid on a photograph, and then copying the image onto my paper a square at a time. I did a portrait of Kennedy like that.

I realized what an illustrator was when I saw paintings like the ones by Norman Rockwell in *Life* magazine. Ads in my comic books for the Famous Artists' School used the word "illustrator," too, so by the time I was nine or ten I had ideas about becoming one.

My mother used to take me to the congregation with her and I remember doing a drawing on the spot of the people in front of me and of the speaker. She showed it around and one of the ladies kept the drawing. Years later, when I was married, mother went to visit the lady and she still had that drawing. In school I filled my notebooks with drawings and I wouldn't get good grades for that. The teachers didn't like it when they found my notebooks.

I was born in New York, but we moved to Puerto Rico when I was ten.

When I was about twelve, I sent a letter to the Famous Artists' School, which I knew from my comic books. You had to do a little test that they sent to see if you had talent. They actually sent somebody to my house. His name was Mr. Azizi and he was a cartoonist for a local newspaper. He told my mother I had some talent but I was too young to sign up at that time. I never studied with the Famous Artists' School, but for the first time I felt that I could be an artist.

In those days there was a government program where you could learn commercial art while in high school. So starting in tenth grade I studied art—not the normal art class you take one hour a week, this was three to four hours a day every day. I studied everything from photography to silkscreening to advertising.

Later, I got a job in a college graphics department. After three years there I realized I wasn't really doing much illustration. I moved back to the States and accidentally found a job at a TV station when I walked into the wrong office with my portfolio. It was crazy. They just happened to be looking for an artist. I worked there for ten years and got to do everything from short films to building sets. We used puppets and animation and all kinds of illustration for educational programs. I learned a lot about putting concepts together, producing shows, art directing, everything. But in the end, I still just wanted to illustrate.

I came to visit an uncle in New York and went out to as many different magazines and publishing companies as I could (I had contacted them before I came). It looked as though there was a good chance I could get some work. So when I went back to Florida, I sold everything I had and quit my job. I had done a poster for a television miniseries called *Shaka Zulu* for WATO in Atlanta. With the money I made from the poster and what I was owed from my job, I moved to New York.

Still Life. Age 15. Pencil, 8½ x 6½".

"You don't do art for money. That's the number one thing. And number two is, you do it because you love it."   *—Raúl Colón*

Where do you get your ideas?

My ideas come from anything. For instance I used to watch MTV a lot and some of the visual ideas I would get came from some scenes from the videos. Other times, walking down the street I might see something happen that would give me an idea. That's why it's good to be in New York, because it's very stimulating in a visual way.

What is a normal day like for you?

People say that it is hard to be organized if you are working on your own, but illustrators *really* have to be disciplined.

I get up at 8 A.M., maybe earlier, and have breakfast and read *The New York Times*. Around 9:30 I come down to my studio and, as I slowly begin to feel like I'm waking up, I pick up whatever job I have for that day. Today, for instance, I'm doing sketches for a new book. So I'll pick up the manuscript and start right where I left off. I work at least until noon and then take a break for an hour or so. Afterward, I will start again and work until dinnertime. When I finish dinner I usually watch a little TV and then by 8 P.M. I'm back at work until it's time for the late news. That's the end of the day. I clean up. And I have to take out the garbage.

Where do you work?

I live in a condominium that is three stories high. Most of the bedrooms are upstairs. The living room and the kitchen are on the main floor. Downstairs in the basement is where my studio is, and there are two glass doors that lead out to a patio. So in the morning I go downstairs, lock the door, and get to work. From my desk I can look out of the window and see the backyard.

Do you have any children? Any pets?

My wife Edie and I have two kids, Brian and Brandon. They are teenagers and both of them are very into sports.

What do you enjoy drawing the most?

Actually, people are number one. I enjoy drawing the human shape, the form. With children's books I can only fool around with the figure a little bit because usually the art must be straightforward. I like to mix it up so I am busy with books, but I also do posters and book covers and illustrations for businesses.

I actually do a lot of editorial work, like work for magazines. It can be fun because you can do whatever you want. I'll be given a news clipping or a magazine article and the client will want me to do my own interpretation of it. It also can be difficult because they want everything finished yesterday. Wow! Now that I think about it, I guess I am rather busy.

Do you ever put people you know in your pictures?

Once in a while I have used my wife Edie as a reference. But even though I use her sometimes to model, I don't make the characters look exactly like her.

What do you use to make your pictures?

The type of paper that I use is very important to me. I use Fabriano watercolor paper because it has a certain texture that I like. It has to be strong enough so that when I really soak it with water it doesn't warp a lot. Even though I tape the paper to the table when I work, it can warp.

I always paint a wash of watercolor to start, usually a yellowish one, but a very monochromatic wash, with not a lot of color in it. On top of that, I will do a sketch, drawing in the figures or whatever the scene calls for. Then I build it up wash after wash, one on top of the other. I gradually darken the areas that I want to be dark. Then I etch into the paper, using something called a scratcher. Finally, I use colored pencil to fill in everything.

How did you get to do your first book?

I got a call from an editor named Anne Schwartz, who asked if I did books. She had seen my artwork in *The New York Times* or somewhere and she wanted to see if I could illustrate a book. She sent me a manuscript and asked me if I would please do one drawing of a scene from the story. I agreed and went ahead and did a drawing so that Ann could see how I would handle it. When she saw the finished piece of artwork, she said, "That's it, go ahead!"

I had never done a book before but I had done lots of storyboards when I was working on animated films at the TV station. It was the same thing. I had to break the story down into different scenes. I submitted my sketches and they were approved. In fact, they said that I basically got it right off the bat. That first book, written by Sharon Dennis Wyeth, was called *Always My Dad*.

Always My Dad by Sharon Dennis Wyeth. 1995. Watercolor, colored pencils, and litho pencils, 11x14". Published by Knopf.

Lisa Desimini

BIRTHDAY: March 21, 1964
Lisa Desimini

MY STORY

I was born in Brooklyn, New York, and we moved a lot. We went from an apartment to a house, then to suburban Long Island, to Florida for three years, back to Brooklyn, then finally to New Jersey for my high-school years. Drawing helped me through the adjustment time in each new place. It made me very comfortable and happy to be alone.

I don't know what came over me but when I was ten years old I went to look for something big to draw on so I could really get into it. I found flat pieces of cardboard, the kind that you fold into a box, and some markers. Since we lived in Florida, we had big beach towels with large bright images. My favorite was a Tom and Jerry cartoon, with the cat on a diving board and the mouse, Jerry, with a saw, getting ready to cut it down. I loved the colors and the shapes and expressions on their faces. So I sat down and copied it. I had so much fun that I haven't stopped. I copied images from cards and books and towels until I got older and started drawing out of my head, which is the most fun for me because I can make things up and add a touch of magic if I want.

In school I was always in charge of the artwork: making posters, decorating for dances, helping friends with their homework. I once painted a sunflower for a friend. It was for her homework, so I signed her name to it. Her mother liked it so much she framed it and hung it up in their living room. My friend and I both thought this was funny and it was great to see my art framed.

My mother, father, teachers, relatives, and friends all told me I should be an artist. Now, this was a lot of support. So I thought, "I am good, I will be an artist." After that if anyone told me I couldn't or shouldn't I only tried harder.

In high school I did the cover of our graduation book. I did get nervous when I realized everyone was going to see it. It made me work a lot harder so I wouldn't be embarrassed. It made me grow up a little. I realized that even though art is fun, it is also serious and important to me. I went to my guidance counselor when I was in tenth grade to talk about colleges. I remember they had a box full of information on many different careers. I looked up "artist" and read that an illustrator paints or draws images for articles in magazines and books. I knew that was what I wanted to do.

I started taking evening art classes with a woman who lived in a beautiful old Tudor home. She was an older woman with a crooked spine and a great collection of music. There were self-portraits all over her walls. This fascinated me, especially the fact that she wasn't married. I didn't know anyone over the age of thirty who wasn't married. I loved being there. It was a small class and I learned to use watercolors, acrylics, charcoal, and pen and ink. But mostly it helped me begin to pay attention to what I loved and what I wanted to surround myself with.

I went to the School of Visual Arts (SVA) in New York City. It was hard to adjust to being back in the city, but it was a great place to be with all of the galleries, museums, movies, and artists. Most of my teachers were working illustrators. Hearing about their jobs and experiences helped a lot. I learned to use oil paints, which became my favorite medium.

I can see now that everything I loved when I was growing up—reading, drawing, painting, playing teacher, and playing with kids—is all part of being a children's book author and illustrator. I have even been back to SVA as a teacher.

Untitled.
Age 12.
Linoleum cut, 7 x 9".

"Keep looking for what
makes you happy. Draw
what feels right. Eat
what feels right."
—*Lisa Desimini*

Where do you get your ideas?

I sit or lie down and try to clear my thoughts. I do a quick search through the images that immediately come to mind. Something will click and get me excited. I will see a little scene or situation, then I start to sketch and write and expand on it. A lot of times I push that first idea away because it seems too weird, but I usually wind up going back to it. Sometimes if I have a book on my mind but I can't get to it because I'm working on something else, I'll dream about it. This happened with the first three spreads of *The Great Peace March* by Holly Near.

What is a normal day like?

I wake up between 7 and 9 A.M. I like the fact that every day is different. I go to the gym or out to breakfast, watch a little TV, or hang out with my boyfriend, who is also an artist and doesn't always have to rush off to work.

We live in Greenwich Village and my studio is in SoHo, which is a ten to fifteen minute walk. Sometimes I run, sometimes I take a cab. Then I'm either sketching, painting, collaging, making three-dimensional images, or writing. I'm also writing bills, sending checks, and making calls. I have a few friends who are illustrators, too, so we talk a lot on the phone, especially when I don't feel like working.

There are many great restaurants in the neighborhood where we meet for dinner at the end of the day around 7 P.M.

Where do you work?

I worked at home for many years. This is the first time I have had a separate studio and I like it very much. I like my studio to be very comfortable. It has a couch, a bed, and a rocking chair. If I have to work late I can sleep there. I'm on a very busy corner in SoHo, on the fourth floor with five windows. I put my desk in the corner so I have two views. I love and need the light and to see people and cars and kids and dogs all the time. It makes me happy. I'm quiet and alone but not lonely.

Do you have any children? Any pets?

I don't have children yet. I would like to have two or three, and twins would be great. A dog, too.

What do you enjoy drawing the most?

I love to draw houses. I draw them every chance I get. The first book I wrote was about a cat looking for a new home. The third book was called *My House*. And now I have a new idea: if an animal had a home, what would it look like? I want to make those houses three-dimensionally.

Do you ever put people you know in your pictures ?

Not consciously, but often the characters wind up looking like me and my family.

What do you use to make your pictures?

I started out using oil paints and after twelve books in that medium I began to get bored. I tried experimenting with different media. For some reason collage clicked and turned out to be perfect for my next book. I did *My House* using magazines and my own photographs and some paint.

After that book, I decided to take a break from my work and go to cooking school for four months. I loved baking bread. I was so inspired that I decided to try working with Sculpey, which is like clay; you bake it in the oven. I made many three-dimensional images for the book *Love Letters* using Sculpey and other materials. I try to do different styles for each book I illustrate.

I have used my computer to work on three books. In *Love Letters,* I photographed the Sculpey objects I had made, scanned them into the computer, added backgrounds, blurred areas, changed colors, etc. For *Tulip Sees America,* I scanned in half-finished paintings, then used the computer to paint, blur, and play around with the size and shape of the images. In *Doodle Dandies,* I used my own photographs, papers, fabric, painted textures, and little sculptures that I made to create collages in the computer. I am having so much fun because I can combine many different techniques in one book project and I never get bored.

How did you get to do your first book?

Children's books were an accident for me. I was out of school for six months trying to do magazine and book cover illustration. I was referred to someone at HarperCollins Publishers, and when I got there I found out it was the children's book department. I thought I was wasting my time, but the editor was interested and asked me to do a couple of paintings for a story called *Heron Street.* I was still skeptical but couldn't turn down the opportunity.

Love Letters by Arnold Adoff. 1997. Mixed media, 20 x 10¼".
Published by Scholastic.

In the month that it took to find out that I had the job, I went to a bookstore and looked at many children's books. I got very excited by the many beautiful books in many different styles. This is how I began to educate myself. The illustrator has a big part in the design of a book and there is a very specific format. By the time I finished that project I was in love. I have been doing children's books ever since and I have written a few, too.

Jane Dyer

BIRTHDAY: March 7, 1949
Jane Dyer

MY STORY

I did not always know I wanted to be an illustrator. As a child, I enjoyed drawing but never thought of myself as an artist. I have a twin sister whose artistic talents have always amazed me. What I loved most was spending hours creating my own imaginary worlds. I especially liked rainy days because it meant I could stay inside and draw, or look at my picture books, or daydream, or play my favorite game—dress-up.

We had a playhouse in our basement with an old wardrobe filled with dress-up clothes that my mother had saved from her childhood. She would also sew anything we designed. Even our dog and cat could not escape being dressed in costume. Since they looked so good in formal wear, I decided to start a school for them and try to teach them to write. They were not fond of their clothes or their lessons and I still have the scars to prove it. But I think I have always preferred animals in proper attire.

Perhaps even greater than any artistic ability I might have had was my imagination. We had a chart on our playhouse wall called "The Land of Make-Believe." I would trace the paths with my finger and get lost in forests, in castles, or in the midst of storybook characters.

When I was growing up I often felt that I could climb right into the illustrations on the pages of our picture books. We didn't have a lot of these books, and the books we had did not have a lot of illustrations, and the illustrations did not have a lot of colors. But when my mother read to me, which she did every night, I would eagerly wait, page after page, for her to turn to an illustration. Then I would study it closely. One of my favorite pictures was in an old set of books called *My Book House*. It was by Maud and Miska Petersham and featured a checkerboard floor. This vision has always been so vivid in my mind that it might be the reason I often put checkerboard floors in my books.

I continued to love the illustrations in children's books through high school and college. At the same time my early interest in teaching remained strong. So I studied elementary education and fine arts in college and went on to teach second grade and kindergarten. It was the parents of my students, along with family and friends, who encouraged me to pursue illustration.

I left teaching after a few years and found a job in Boston writing and illustrating teachers' guides for a K–3 reading program which was being developed by Pleasant Rowland (who later founded the American Girls Collection). She said she thought there was a guardian angel on her shoulder the day I walked in. I think perhaps it was the other way around. I left when my first daughter was born, but kept working freelance at home.

One day I was asked to illustrate a poem in full color for the third-grade textbook. I pulled the playpen up to my drawing table and continued working on textbooks for many years, eventually with two daughters growing up by my side. This was my training for eight years, for both illustrating and motherhood.

I feel very fortunate to be able to illustrate children's books and be at home with my family. It is as if every day is a rainy day from my childhood and I am allowed to stay inside and color in my own imaginary world.

Portrait of Mrs. Erber (my kindergarten teacher who had large hips). Age 5. Crayon, 12 x 9".

"Spend some time each day dreaming."
— *Jane Dyer*

Where do you get your ideas?

My work is a combination of memories from my childhood (the rich colors and intricate patterns of the vintage clothes that I wore for playing dress-up are with me still); images of my daughters as they grew (I'll never forget how cuddly they were in their pajamas with feet, or how enchanting they looked with garlands of flowers in their hair); and pictures from favorite books I've collected over the years, including those illustrated by artists I consider my mentors: Jessie Willcox Smith (for her images of home), Maxfield Parrish (for his design sense), Carl Larsson (for his scenes of family), and Maud and Miska Petersham (for their whimsy).

What is a normal day like for you?

I get up about 6:30 each morning. While my youngest daughter gets ready for school, I take care of feeding the pets: Woolly, our Wheaton terrier, three cats, two lovebirds, and a lily pond full of goldfish. I take a cup of chamomile tea to my studio, which is in our house. I like to be in the studio early, even if the house is not quite in order. Once there, I plug in a garland of little white party lights to make it festive, put on some music, and begin my day. I work until my daughter gets home, and then we visit for a while. I go back to the studio and work until it is time for dinner. I enjoy cooking, but not grocery shopping, so I have to figure out what there is in the kitchen and be pretty creative. I think I'm fairly good at it.

After dinner I try to walk for about an hour along Mill River, which runs by the border of Smith College. Maxfield Parrish once wrote that only in New England was the sky the color he painted it. I often get to witness that sky on my walks. I no longer work at night as I had done for many years, but I often return to my studio late at night to look at the paintings I am working on, especially if I feel they are going well. Then I like to get in bed and either watch a movie or read.

Where do you work?

I work in a sun-filled studio. Beyond my desk are French doors that open onto a terrace, gardens, and lily pond designed by my husband, a landscape architect. I enjoy the solitude of observing the changing seasons as I work. My work area is surrounded by bookshelves filled with the books I so often use for inspiration and reference. One wall is filled with pictures of my children, as well as cards and messages they and other friends have given me over the years.

Do you have any children? Any pets?

I have two daughters. Brooke loves horses, drawing, the outdoors, and her car, a 1972 BMW 2002 that she named Maggie. Cecily loves art and her violin and she has a genuine curiosity about everything. They both started their lives in baby baskets on my drawing table. As I write this, Brooke is in college and Cecily is in high school. It has been a long and joyous road.

Ziggy and Woolly, relaxing in the sun.

Child of Faerie by Jane Yolen. 1997. Watercolor, 11 x 14".
Published by Little, Brown and Co.

What do you enjoy drawing the most?
I like drawing children and animals. I think my favorite is when they can be together in a make-believe companionship, as in *Goldilocks and the Three Bears*. Since I have two daughters, I find I often draw girls.

Do you ever put people you know in your pictures?

Almost everyone in my books is based on someone I know. Friends, family, and even pets are often in my pictures. (No one who visits my house is safe.) Cecily was first, as my inspiration for Goldilocks, although she was only three and hardly had any hair (now she has long, thick, curly red hair). She has appeared in numerous books since then. Brooke, who has long, straight blonde hair, was the "girl in the golden bower." My husband was once given fairy wings and striped socks and has asked not to be used anymore. I believe my friend Barry Moser and my dog Woolly may be tied for being in the most number of books.

What do you use to make your pictures?

I begin by making small thumbnail sketches, about one to two inches in size, on tracing paper using a 2H pencil. Then I make another sketch the same size the book will be. I put that on my light box, cover it with a piece of watercolor paper, and trace it, again with a 2H pencil because they don't smear when I am painting. I tape my watercolor paper onto my drawing table so it will stay flat as I paint. I use brushes that range in size from 000 (very thin) for details to 22 (fairly chunky) for background washes. Every once in a while I add some colored pencils. I have an electric eraser to help with mistakes and to get rid of occasional kitty pawprints.

How did you get to do your first book?

After moving to western Massachusetts, I met Jane Yolen at a writers' workshop which she conducted. I presented my work and she told me that I should take my portfolio into New York to show to children's book publishers.

I had eight appointments in two days and was rejected by the first seven. Then snow got into my portfolio and ruined some of the pieces and my wallet was stolen from my purse. I started crying on the way to my final appointment, thinking I should just go home to my family who loved me. But I met with one more editor who was looking for someone to illustrate a little board book of *Goldilocks and the Three Bears*. I happened to have a sample of just that in my portfolio.

That was in 1983, and I haven't been without a book since. (Thank you, everyone!)

BIRTHDAY: August 28, 1959
Kevin Hawkes

MY STORY

I think I've always loved to do things with my hands. When I was very young, my favorite activities were playing with modeling clay, coloring with crayons, and digging in the dirt with my father's tools. (He was very patient.) Later when I got into school, I found that I really loved to draw. I drew just about everything I could think of: ships, castles, racecars, monsters, and sharks. Art day was my favorite. That's when the art teacher came to our room. It seemed like she came only once a month. Once she drew a picture from her imagination of an elf sitting under a toadstool. That picture got me really excited, and for weeks I was drawing all kinds of make-believe creatures. My family lived in central France when I was five, and many memories of castles with dungeons and winding staircases came back and started getting into my artwork.

My mother arranged for me to take some art lessons with a neighbor. I was introduced to charcoal, pastels, and oil paint. I loved oil paint! I wasn't very good at it but I liked squeezing tubes of color onto the palette and mixing them in different ways. Mom gave me a set of oil paints in a wooden box with a handle. I used them all through school and some of the brushes even lasted into college.

Growing up, I never thought I'd be an artist, I just loved to draw and paint. My first real art education came in the ninth grade when my art teacher, Sherry Hodges, taught my brother and me how to use various media: pen and ink, watercolor, charcoal, pastels, oil paint, and, for the first time, acrylic paint. I was taking a sculpture class also and learning how to model things in clay, plaster, wire, and papier-mâché. I built a life-sized mountaineer out of papier-mâché, complete with a climbing axe. I made him in a sitting position so that when he dried I could take him home on the school bus, which I did, much to my mother's amazement. (She was very patient.)

I got a lot of ideas from the family garage, a storehouse for every type of material imaginable. I could find scraps of wood, leather, wire, balls of string, old typewriters, canoes, beeswax, bowling balls, inner tubes, axe heads, sewing machines, and even a few dirt-clogged tools. I also loved to whittle with my pocketknife. I think I always had at least two Band-Aids on each hand at any given time. I suppose all the sculpting helped me understand how light falls on objects, one of the more important elements in my paintings.

In college I signed up for history and science. (I thought archaeology might be fun, given my experience with the garage.) I took art classes, too, but nothing seemed to grab my attention. Then a friend suggested I take an illustration course. I did, and as soon as I saw the art of N. C. Wyeth, Howard Pyle, Maxfield Parrish, and many other great illustrators, I knew I was hooked.

After college, my first art job was working as an assistant animator producing cartoons for Saturday-morning television. I was horrible! I had my own style and could never make it work with those cartoon characters. After three months I got a new job as a photographic retoucher. It was a good job because I learned how to do fine details in a realistic way.

When my wife, Karen, and I moved to Boston, I looked for any work I could get and ended up in a bookstore in charge of the children's section. For two years I read picture books on every lunch break, studying the artwork. One day, with a portfolio filled with my favorite pieces, I set off to see a publisher to try and do my own books.

My Dog Jenny. Age 10. Pastel, 11½ x 8½".

"Be patient with yourself. If your painting doesn't look quite right, keep trying. And try different things."   —*Kevin Hawkes*

Where do you get your ideas?
I usually just read the story and pretend I'm a fly. I buzz around the scenes in my mind, flying low and flying high to see what catches my eye, especially the light and shadow.

What is a normal day like for you?

I get up early and do something active, work in the garden or ride my bike around the island where I live. (It only takes twenty minutes.) Then I have breakfast with my wife, Karen, and our three children. After I wash the breakfast dishes, I go to work, usually around 9 A.M.

I think best in the morning, so that's when I do sketches and get ideas for my upcoming illustrations. I take a break for lunch at noon and then work on paintings until 5 P.M. After that I usually help fix supper, do homework with my children, or go on a bike ride. In the summer we go to the shore a lot or walk down to the candy store for ice cream.

Where do you work?

I work in a small room on the second floor of our house on Peaks Island. The room is painted green. There is a chair, an easel, a table, and a closet where I keep most of my books and supplies. I like this small room with two windows looking out into the trees because there isn't much to distract me. I have a radio to listen to and get most of the news from there. We don't have a TV.

Do you have any children? Any pets?

Yes, three children. Spencer (10), Jessie, a girl (8), and Ian (4). They all love to draw and read and like to play musical instruments.

What do you enjoy drawing the most?

Enormous objects flying through the air and dramatic shadows.

Do you ever put people you know in your pictures?

Once in a while I will use a model for reference but not normally. Many of the characters I draw are rather distorted, so I'm not sure if any of my friends or family would enjoy being drawn into my picture books.

What do you use to make your pictures?

I use acrylic paint mostly. I have done one or two picture books with oil paints but it dries too slowly for me, so I always come back to acrylics.

Tortilla chips and salsa also play a large part in the creation of my art (late-night snacks!).

How did you get to do your first book?

I got my first book offer when I showed my portfolio to Audrey Bryant, an editor at David Godine Publisher. She offered me a manuscript called *The Turnip* by Walter de la Mere. It is still one of my favorite stories ever.

At almost the same time, I got a telephone call from an art director in New York City named Rachel Simon. Susan Pearson, an editor at Lothrop, Lee and Shepard Books, wanted to see me right away, could I come down?

So Karen and I grabbed a train in the middle of a snowstorm and rushed down to New York from Boston. It was so hectic—at one point Karen had one foot on the platform and one foot on the train, holding it for me while a conductor yelled, "We gotta go, lady!" Finally we made it.

When I walked into Susan Pearson's office she shook my hand and said, "So, you're Kevin Hawkes. I want to be your publisher."

"You do?" I asked. Then I said, "Okay!" And that's how I got my first book, *Then the Troll Heard the Squeak*.

My Little Sister Ate One Hare
by Bill Grossman. 1996.
Acrylic, 11¼ x 9".
Published by Crown.

BIRTHDAY: September 27, 1957

G. Brian Karas

MY STORY

When I was about seven or eight years old, I remember standing on my road on a sunny, windy spring day, wishing I could go somewhere and not being able to. There was a lot of leftover sand from the winter snowplows in drifts on the street. An especially strong wind blew up the hill and with it a lot of airborne sand. When it blew in my face I didn't think, "Yecch, sand in my face." Instead I thought that maybe this sand was being blown all over the world and maybe this sand was just in from the Sahara or Mojave Desert. It made me feel as though I was taking that trip along with that warm sand and for a moment I felt I was airborne, too, traveling all over the world. That's what reading books did (and does) for me, too. They took me to faraway places. There are pictures I can remember from books I read as a child that are still vivid in my mind. They became a part of me.

I can't think back to when I began to draw; it seems like something I always did and enjoyed. My sister gave me what may have been my first art lesson when I was five or so. She taught me how to draw Pilgrims by first drawing a circle, then lines for hair, and finally adding a simple rectangle for a hat. I used to torment her (she's my older sister so it was my duty as younger brother to do that) by drawing funny portraits of her—she didn't care for them at all!

In school I became the "class artist," a distinction I enjoyed. My favorite things to draw were Charles M. Schulz's *Peanuts* characters. They were my heroes. I still can't get through a Christmas season unless I watch *A Charlie*

Brown Christmas. When I was a little older, I drew imaginary ski areas, making up my own trail and lift systems. I vividly envisioned each one as if I were there. I also liked drawing detailed maps of imaginary places. I became a big fan of J. R. R. Tolkien's *Lord of the Rings* trilogy, which may have influenced me.

The idea that I could actually be an artist as a profession didn't occur to me until much later, in high school. I went to art school after high school to learn the skills of drawing and painting. I thought that learning these skills would make me a good artist. But all those classes taught me was how to get my ideas and feelings down on paper or canvas or whatever. It was a very good school. I had excellent teachers who taught me well, but that other part about those ideas and feelings had to come from me. It's easy to make a picture that looks nice, but it has to say something and I felt that I didn't have anything to say. I must have panicked because I didn't really know what I felt like, either.

We had an open assignment class: we could draw or paint anything we wanted. I usually looked at other paintings to get ideas, thinking I could get by if I did my own versions of someone else's ideas. And that was usually what they looked like. Then one night I drew a picture of a very old lady, a hundred-year-old princess, riding a rocking horse in a dark forest. It was nonsense and I don't know where the idea came from, but it reminded me of stories I read as a child. I remember feeling like those characters lost in the dark woods—lonely, scared, but also curious about what was around the corner or behind those big tree trunks and twisted roots.

When I took that idea and started to develop it more fully, it became a story. It then began to occur to me that I would like to be a children's book illustrator. I could take the ideas and feelings I had as a child and still had, create a story, and express that to someone else. It could be meaningful to someone else, and it made me feel good, too.

The idea that maybe my pictures are making an impression on someone else means a great deal to me, and is what compels me to always do what I'm doing— making books for children, and me.

The Mona Karen.
Age 7. Crayon,
3¼ x 4½".

"No work is so dismal that you have to throw it out and start over again. Try to fix it, or paint over it, or cut it in shreds and glue those together to make a great collage."

—*G. Brian Karas*

Where do you get your ideas?

When I'm illustrating a story that someone else has written, my ideas come from the story. That's where some ideas start, at least. From there, I get taken down a sort of path that could lead me anywhere, but it's usually to a place I was when I was young. If I'm illustrating a story about a garden, for instance, I may start to think about the vegetable garden in my childhood backyard, which was up on the hill near the woods with a really spooky old tree that stood too close by. That may remind me of the island we used to walk to at low tide, which had a mysterious stone arch that was covered with wild vines. And from there, who knows. I think I collect all my ideas, and if my memory happens to be working, I can bring those ideas back to the surface.

When I write my own stories to illustrate, I usually try to think back to what I felt most strongly about when I was young. That's not so easy to do. Sometimes I have to listen to children to remember how I used to feel about things. Sometimes I look at children's drawings. They are a good way to look at the world through seven-year-old eyes. And I always look at what's around me—real life, artwork, photographs, movies, books, everything I can.

What is a normal day like for you?

That's a hard question to answer. I just moved from a big city to the country, so I don't know what's normal for me right now. I used to have a studio in a small cottage that I drove to, which was about ten minutes from my house. It was very quiet. Now I am working at home. It is not quiet. It is very *noisy!* A three-year-old and an eight-year-old manage to generate more noise than I ever imagined possible. And I thought moving to the country would be peaceful!

I have a studio at the end of the house and when I look out my window I can see a maple tree that must be a thousand years old. I'm surrounded by books, art supplies, and pictures. I sometimes listen to music or the news (if I'm not trying to think too hard) and when I procrastinate I talk to a friend on the telephone. Mostly what I do is either drawing, painting, reading, or looking for ideas. There's also a lot of paperwork to do but I won't talk about that.

Where do you work?

I work at home in a room that used to be half the garage. I'm not sure I like it yet. I don't miss driving to work, but when I work at home it's very easy to become distracted. For instance, when I look out my window and see the broken gutter that needs fixing, or when I hear my kids having more fun than I think I am and I want to join them. I have a nice view from my windows and I try to get out of the house at least once a day so I don't live in my pajamas.

Do you have any children? Any pets?

I have two boys. Bennett is eight and Zachary is three. They are the joy of my life, and they make me crazy. We have an Airedale terrier named Buddy.

What do you enjoy drawing the most?

I like drawing many things. I like drawing things that make me laugh. But I suppose if you really want to know, the things I enjoy drawing most are funny-looking dogs and ridiculous-looking people.

I like art to move me somewhere—to a different country or planet or neighborhood. Or to make me feel what it's like to be someone or something else, such as a sea captain or a thundercloud, or a snail.

Buddy . . . his name says it all.

Do you ever put people you know in your pictures?
Yes, but I'm not telling who they are or what pictures they're in. When I was in the third grade I got into big trouble for drawing pictures of my teacher. She found them not at all flattering. Now I just let people guess. It's safer.

What do you use to make your pictures?
Gouache, which is a little like poster paint and it's pronounced "gwäsh," acrylic

Sleepless Beauty
by Frances Minters.
1996. Gouache,
acrylic, and pencil,
17¼ x 10½".
Published by
Viking.

paint, and pencils. When making a collage I have been known to use anything I can glue down.

How did you get to do your first book?

I'll bet that my persistent behavior had something to do with it. I work very hard to get what I want. Maybe I don't always get it when I want it, but I think the things you really want are worth every bit of your persistence, and I'll bet a lot of grownups are wishing I hadn't said that.

B. Lewin

BIRTHDAY: May 12, 1937
Betsy Lewin

MY STORY

I've always loved to draw. Except for a brief desire to be a pirate, I've never wanted to be anything but an artist. The first drawings I can remember are the ones I drew on the blank pages and in the margins of my storybooks.

My mother bought a set of books for my brother and me called _My Book House_. There were twelve leatherbound volumes starting with Mother Goose nursery rhymes and moving on to fairy tales, folktales, stories from foreign lands, and stories about history and adventure. They were full of beautiful illustrations including some by Kate Greenaway and Randolph Caldecott. I still have those books, and they still inspire me.

Besides drawing in books, I drew on paper bags and napkins and on any old scraps of paper I could find. In fact, I still do. The things I liked to draw best as a child were horses, elephants, fish, and people peeking out from behind trees—oh, and pirates. Even today when I'm drawing for my own pleasure, or developing characters for a new story, I find that my old childhood favorites keep popping up on paper and sometimes find their way into my books.

I loved Ernest Shepard's drawings of Winnie the Pooh and his friends. Shepard got so much personality and gesture into his characters with simple, black pen lines. I really liked movies, especially cowboy movies (I studied the way the horses looked) and cartoons. The exaggerated gestures and expressions appealed to me. Walt Disney's animals had a special magic. They were cartoons, but I could see the real animal in them.

In school everyone asked me to draw pictures for them. I especially liked to do caricatures. I began to write, too. I would write little stories and illustrate them. Even then I guess I knew that what I really wanted to do was write and illustrate books. At home I had an easel and painted in oils. Our local hardware and paint store supplied me with stretched canvases, paints, and brushes. Sometimes I would paint from life, but mostly I worked from my imagination.

Every summer I entered my work in the art exhibit at the county fair. I always won blue ribbons. I sold my first painting when I was fourteen. A local lawyer bought it for his daughter. It was an oil portrait of a doe-eyed girl with a solemn expression. I painted it from my imagination.

My grade-school, junior-high, and private art teachers all encouraged me to further my art education. My parents thought it was wonderful that I could draw, but they did not want me to go to art school. They said it would be hard to make a living as an artist (maybe even harder than being a pirate). I didn't know anyone who was making a living as an artist, and it was a little scary to think about.

But it was scarier to think about not going to art school. What else would I do? My parents finally agreed to let me go. It was like closing my eyes, holding my nose, and jumping into the deep end of the pool for the first time, but I did it. And here I am.

Figure on Horseback.
Age 5. Pencil,
6 x 9".

"Draw in your own way,
from your own heart."
—*Betsy Lewin*

Where do you get your ideas?

My ideas come from the things I see and experiences that I have. I love animals, so my ideas usually involve at least one animal. Sometimes ideas pop into my head from out of the blue. This usually happens in the middle of the night. I jump out of bed and grope my way through the dark (being careful not to step on a cat) into my studio, where I quickly jot down my thoughts or sketches. The next morning I look at my notes and decide whether or not there really is a good idea for a book there.

Sometimes ideas come from my travels to Africa, India, and other exotic places. I got the idea for *Booby Hatch* while observing blue-footed boobies on the Galápagos Islands. *Chubbo's Pool* is based on my personal experience with a selfish hippopotamus that I met in Botswana. *What's the Matter, Habibi?* was inspired by my encounters with camels and camel drivers in Egypt and Morocco.

What is a normal day like for you?

I usually get up between 6 and 7 A.M. and feed Slick and Chopper. Then I go to the corner luncheonette for breakfast. This gets me out of the house for some fresh air and a chat with neighbors before going to work in my studio, which is on the second floor of my brownstone house in Brooklyn.

Between 8 and 1 o'clock, I am involved in whatever book I'm working on, either reading a manuscript, doing research or sketches, or making the finished drawings. The rest of the day I tend to everyday chores like doing laundry (ugh!) or watering plants, which is pleasant.

Some days I go to the gym to exercise, and then go to a movie. In the evening I always take time to play with Slick and Chopper. They like to chase string and attack shoelaces.

Where do you work?

My formal workplace is my studio. That's where my drawing table and art supplies are, and where I surround myself with things that I love to look at and that inspire me—souvenirs from my travels, pictures and objects that appeal to me. But it seems that I'm always working. No matter where I am, I'm always looking for a story to tell in pictures.

Do you have any children? Any pets?

No children. My books are my children. My husband, Ted, and I have two spoiled cats, Slick and Chopper. They keep life interesting.

What do you enjoy drawing the most?

Animals. They come in so many wonderful shapes and sizes. I love the way they move, from the graceful cat to the lumbering hippo to the skittering crab.

Do you ever put people you know in your pictures?

Not really, but I often have someone that I know in mind when I'm developing a character, like a tall, thin uncle of mine, or one of my grandmothers.

Chopper relaxing.

What do you use to make your pictures?

Usually I draw with a brush or a felt-tip pen on tracing paper. Then I photocopy the drawings onto one-ply Strathmore bristol paper and add watercolor washes. When I paint in a more naturalistic style, I still draw on tracing paper, but with a hard 4H pencil. Then I transfer the drawing to a heavier four- or five-ply Strathmore paper and paint in watercolors. I use photo reference when I work this way.

What's the Matter, Habibi?
1997. Watercolor, 15½ x 10".
Published by Clarion Books.

How did you get to do your first book?

An editor at Dodd, Mead and Company saw a poem called "Cat Count" that I wrote and illustrated for *Humpty Dumpty,* a children's magazine, and asked me to expand it into a thirty-two-page picture book. I did all the drawings, including the cover, in black-and-white brush line. It's still my favorite drawing tool, and *Cat Count* is still one of my favorite books.

BIRTHDAY: May 6, 1935
Ted Lewin

MY STORY

I think you are born an artist. You don't have much choice in the matter. I've always loved to draw and used to sit alone by the hour drawing in the sun-drenched parlor at the back of our old frame house in Buffalo, New York. Sometimes I'd copy the work of the great illustrators and painters. Once, when I was eleven years old, I did a portrait in oils of Harry Truman. I sent it to him and received a letter of praise from the White House.

We had many exotic pets when I was a kid: a lion named Sheba, a chimp named Jago, and many kinds of monkeys. Our rhesus monkey, named Cheeta, loved to go for rides with me on my bike. She would sit straddling the back of my neck holding onto my hair. If I stopped for too long she would pull my hair, shaking my head back and forth. Once she got loose and led us on a wild chase as she jumped from tree to tree. We finally lured her down from a church steeple with Cheerios, her favorite snack.

Our neighbors called us "the circus people." I think being surrounded by all these creatures is where I developed my love of drawing animals. One day I made dozens of drawings of Jago as he slept on our front porch. He was less than a year old and had huge, floppy ears. He woke up, took one look at the drawings, and promptly bit me.

At least my parents, two brothers, and sister liked my drawings and encouraged me. I was the only one in my family who could draw. My parents thought that I had been given a wonderful gift. They wanted to send me for art lessons at the museum on Saturday mornings, but my eighth-grade art teacher talked them out of it. He said it was better to let my natural abilities develop on their own. Instructions could come later. So I drew and drew and drew.

And I read. I read all the Edgar Rice Burroughs *Tarzan* books, and I read stories about exotic places—about jungles in Africa where there were gorillas, great plains jam-packed with animals, forests in India where tigers roamed. And I longed to see all these things for myself.

My high-school art teacher was a graduate of Pratt Institute in Brooklyn, and I was her prize pupil. In fact, I was the only serious student in class. She encouraged me to go to Pratt. I needed money for school so, at seventeen, I became a professional wrestler and joined my brother, Donn, in Ohio as his tag team partner. That summer we wrestled all over the Midwest and in the fall I was on my way to art school in the big city. I continued wrestling two or three nights a week all through school and for ten years after as a kind of part-time job.

At Pratt came all the instruction I could handle. I learned anatomy, composition, and color. I learned how to really paint in oils, and I learned how to really see. I carried a sketchbook with me everywhere I went, and I drew and drew and drew.

In one of my classes, we were told to make a picture and write a "statement" to go with it. In doing that assignment I learned how pictures and words can work together to tell a story.

Many of my childhood dreams have come true. I'm traveling and seeing the world and, best of all, I'm sharing it all with readers.

Lion. Age 10. Ink and watercolor, 6 x 9".

"Carry a sketchbook and draw."
—*Ted Lewin*

Where do you get your ideas?

Ideas come from all over the place. I got the idea for *Tiger Trek* while sitting on the back of an elephant in India. The idea for *Sacred River* came while I was sitting at sunrise in a creaky old rowboat on the Ganges in India. The idea for *Market* came while riding on a subway train in New York City following a journey to the mountains of Ecuador.

What is a normal day like for you?

I get up at 7 A.M. every day. Because I work at home I go out to a local luncheonette for breakfast. That gets me out of the house for a while before I start work. At 8 A.M. I start work and work until 1 or 2 P.M. I'm very disciplined about this and I hardly ever take a break. After five or six hours, my eyes are tired and my thinking is no longer sharp. So I stop and do something different. Usually, I go to the gym and exercise for a couple of hours. I work almost every day, but if I feel stale I take a day off and go bird watching or hiking in the woods.

Where do you work?

I live in a 117-year-old brownstone row house in Brooklyn. My studio is on the top floor. It is one big room. I draw and paint there, and it doubles as a photography studio.

Do you have any children? Any pets?

Betsy and I don't have children, but we are like proud parents every time we send a finished book off to a publisher. We have two fat cats, Slick and Chopper, that keep us pretty busy.

What do you enjoy drawing the most?

I love to draw, period. I especially like the challenge of drawing animals and birds.

Do you ever put people you know in your pictures?

I use my friends and neighbors many times for the characters in the books I illustrate. Sometimes I even sneak myself in there. In my book *Fair*, I'm testing my strength trying to ring the bell in the carnival scene.

What do you use to make your pictures?

I work in watercolor on Strathmore bristol paper. I make a very careful drawing first using a 5H pencil. When that is exactly the way I want it, I begin to apply the watercolor as freely as I can. I work from photo research that I've taken on location myself or photographed in my studio, or from my picture reference collection. I'm careful to get everything to look as real and correct as I can.

Slick in my studio.

Fair. 1997. Watercolor, 21½ x 9". Published by Lothrop, Lee & Shepard Books.

How did you get to do your first book?

For many years I did jacket art and black-and-white interior illustrations for young adult books. I was always intrigued by the picture book format of telling a story with sequential pictures. So when Houghton Mifflin offered me a manu-

script called *Faithful Elephants* I jumped at the chance. It is a true story of what happens to innocent creatures in wartime. I was very moved by the story and thought illustrating it would help children understand what a terrible thing war is. I think I was asked to illustrate it because I love to draw animals, and because I use real people for models I can get great feeling into my figures.

BIRTHDAY: January 20, 1959
Keiko Narahashi

MY STORY

As a child I spent a lot of time drawing. When I was four or five I had some Japanese fairy-tale books that I loved. I spent hours copying illustrations of the beautiful princess who lived on the moon (my favorite story). I tried hard to draw her face just like in the picture. I loved the way she looked, drawn simply, as shown here.

I practiced over and over, trying to get the lines just right so my princess would be as beautiful as the one in the book. I learned a lot about drawing by copying those pictures, like how to simplify complicated shapes—you don't have to put in every single detail. Even now I draw faces the same way!

I was born in Tokyo, Japan, and my family—my mother, father, and younger brother, Taro—moved to the United States when I was six. I started first grade in a new school in a new country. I didn't know one word of English! My teacher tried to teach me the names of colors by pointing to crayons and saying, "Red, blue, purple . . ."

I loved school, but it was frustrating not to be able to communicate easily with classmates. Sometimes, I got into trouble because I had to *do* things to express my feelings. When a boy took my shoes to tease me, I didn't know how to say, "Please give my shoes back." So I chased him, grabbed my shoes, and hit him with one. I was so mad! This wasn't the right way to behave, but frustration can lead to things like that. That year, I got an F in conduct on my report card.

But speaking English didn't matter in art. *That* was a different story. I was on equal footing when it came to lines, colors, and shapes. This was a "language" that I—and everyone else—understood. In fact, I was on better than equal footing because of the hours I'd spent practicing those princesses. It was much easier to express myself with a crayon or a paintbrush. When I drew, I didn't worry about finding the right words or doing the wrong thing; I felt confident and focused. I felt great!

I drew and painted all through childhood, long after I had mastered English. For a while I drew only horses (palominos were my favorite). I wrote and illustrated stories, mostly about wild horses with mountain lions as the bad guys. Later, I drew teenage girls in neat outfits. It was the early 1970s so my fashion drawings showed bell bottoms, "peasant" blouses, beaded headbands, and long, long hair—very funny-looking now, but then I thought it looked fantastic!

In fourth grade I entered a poster contest that aimed to bring supporters together for a new zoo. Working to come up with an idea for my first illustration assignment, I found I was pretty good at problem solving. It was a lot of fun and I won. I was extremely proud of my poster, and even today I still think it looks terrific! But it was the sense of knowing how to handle such a challenge, rather than the winning, that stayed with me.

At ten, it hadn't occurred to me that drawing could be a career, but the contest helped me realize what I was good at and what I enjoyed most. I later thought about being a fashion illustrator, but I got tired of just drawing fashionable girls. Not until I had children of my own did I start thinking back on how I copied illustrations from my favorite picture books and how much it had meant to me. It seemed natural as an adult to try making my own picture books.

Today I still spend a lot of time drawing, just as I did as a child. Drawing and painting still do for me what it did for me back then as a confused first-grader in a strange, new country—it helps me to figure out who I am and to communicate with the world.

Where do you get your ideas?

Most of my picture ideas come from everyday things, things so common you don't even notice they're there. Like shadows. You don't always see them, but you would definitely notice if shadows were missing, especially on a sunny day. The world would look very strange without shadows!

I became so fascinated with shadows that my first book, *I Have a Friend,* was about them. I was driving and looking at the shadows of trees on the side of the road. As it got later in the afternoon, the shadows stretched out farther across the road as though they were trying to reach the other side. That made me think about how shadows constantly changed shape and size throughout the day. My book started from one simple, everyday image and grew from there.

Zoo Parade. Age 10. Crayon and pencil, 28 x 22".

"If you love to draw, draw a lot of what you love to draw. Look hard at the things that fascinate you and don't pay too much attention to advice about drawing, especially from grownups, like me."   —*Keiko Narahashi*

What is a normal day like for you?

I never seem to have "normal" days, *but* on a typical day, I wake up around 7:30 A.M. and *rush rush rush* around the apartment with my husband, Peter, and our children, Micah and Joy, to get us all to where we're supposed to be on time. Peter goes to the hospital (he's a pediatrician), Micah goes to middle school, Joy goes to her elementary school, and I go to my studio.

Once I get to my studio around 10 A.M., I sit and look out my window where I have a beautiful view of the Manhattan skyline. I drink coffee and look out the window some more. Eventually, I start my working day. I might work on some large paintings on canvas or on illustrations for my latest book. Usually, I stay at my studio until 4 P.M. or so, but since I live in New York City, I might also spend time going to museums, galleries, libraries, and book shops to do research on whatever I'm working on. What a great job!

Then, I pick up Joy from her afterschool and go home (Peter and Micah get home on their own) where we all *rush rush rush* around cooking dinner, doing homework, cleaning up, reading stories, etc., until bedtime.

Sometimes I get crabby about all the rushing around I do, but I try to remember how lucky I am to get to do both the rushing and the sitting still. You can't really appreciate one without the other!

Where do you work?

I work mostly at my studio, which is a big room in an old factory building in New York. The factory is no longer in operation and is now occupied by artists like me. I also work at home at a small desk in the corner of my bedroom, especially when I am working on the final art for a book. This way I can work in my pajamas.

Do you have any children? Any pets?

Yes. Micah is thirteen and likes to skateboard and Joy is seven. She likes animals. They both like to draw. We also have two snakes, Caramel and Sprinkles, and a guinea pig named Patina.

What do you enjoy drawing the most?

I like to draw children best, and also animals. My least favorite things to draw are room interiors.

Do you ever put people you know in your pictures?

Yes, my son, Micah, is in *I Have a Friend,* and Joy is the little girl in *Is That Josie?* I also "borrow" from different people I know; for example, the way someone stands, or the way a child might play with an umbrella.

What do you use to make your pictures?

I use watercolor and gouache paints on D'Arches paper, a nice, thick paper

I Have a Friend.
1987. Watercolor, 16 x 11".
Published by Margaret K. McElderry Books.

made specially for watercolor paints. It's much stronger than regular drawing paper so it doesn't wrinkle when you put a lot of paint or water on it.

How did you get to do your first book?

I was home with my baby thirteen years ago and had some time on my hands, so I wrote and illustrated the first version of *I Have a Friend*. I took it around to publishers and the third person I met, Margaret McElderry, offered to publish it.

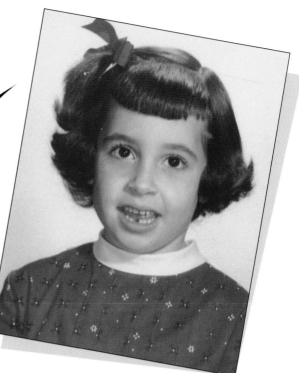

ℰ𝓁𝒾𝓈ℯ 𝒫𝓇𝒾𝓂𝒶𝓋ℯ𝓇𝒶

BIRTHDAY: May 19, 1955
Elise Primavera

MY STORY

When I was about six years old my brother was the best artist I knew. He taught me how to draw a tree. He said, "If you can do this: then you can draw a tree!" After I mastered the tree he taught me how to draw this:

Soon after that I began to copy cartoons from comic books. I was hooked. I loved to draw! I drew on everything, the insides of my school books (which I wasn't supposed to do), my desks (which I wasn't supposed to do). I drew on my other hand, I even drew on my clothes. I especially liked to draw on my pants. Once I drew on my raincoat while I was sitting on the school bus. For that I got into a lot of trouble!

I can't say that I ever dreamed I'd grow up to be an artist. I think the real reason that I am one today is because of the rheumatic fever I got at the end of fifth grade. I was confined to my bed for an entire summer and given three large paperback books: *Learn to Draw Animals, Learn to Draw Flowers,* and *Learn to Draw People.* All summer I practiced. By the time I left my sickbed I could draw a really good orchid, a goat, and a horse head. I don't remember if I learned to draw a person, so I probably didn't.

My parents had a giant book of reproductions of paintings by Michelangelo. In it were images of the angels and saints that he painted on the ceiling of the

Sistine Chapel, in Italy. I spent a lot of time looking at these and trying to draw the figures. I think that was the beginning of my interest in drawing people.

Still, it never occurred to me that I would be an artist. An artist was like Michelangelo, not like me! My main focus then was on horses. I had been riding since I was eight; by the time I was thirteen we had moved to a small farm and had a couple of horses and ponies, two donkeys, and two dogs. I wanted to be a vet, or better yet, a famous horseback rider!

During that time my drawing took a back seat. I put all my energy into riding. Even becoming a vet began to pale in comparison to what I really wanted—to ride in the Olympics! All throughout high school I kept this goal in mind. When it came time for college I wanted to stay home and ride full time. My parents insisted that I try at least two years of college. So we compromised. I went to art school in Philadelphia and commuted home to ride on weekends. What ensued was a tug of war between my riding and my artwork.

After college I was at a real crossroads: would I continue riding and try to make a living at it, or would I pursue a career in art? It took me two years to decide. I was living near Chadd's Ford, Pennsylvania, at the time and was very confused about what to do next. I remember I had decided to visit the local art museum, which just happened to be the wonderful Brandywine River Museum.

As I moved from one painting to the next by Howard Pyle and his students N. C. Wyeth, Jessie Willcox Smith, and many others, my confusion disappeared. It became very clear to me that what I wanted to do was something like these paintings I was seeing. It was there that I made up my mind.

It's been a long road from that moment to where I am now, but it just confirms my belief in the power of art. It changed my life, and I'm glad it did. But U.S. Olympic Committee, if you're listening and there's an extra spot on you equestrian team, I wouldn't say no!

Where do you get your ideas?

I get my ideas from everywhere—conversations, books I'm reading, movies, or just walking down the street and looking at what's around me. Whatever I'm working on is with me twenty-four hours a day, even when I'm asleep. I get some great ideas from my dreams.

One thing that doesn't work is if I sit down and say okay, *now,* I need to think up an idea. Oh, idea? Yoohoo? Are you there? Usually I am doing something else, like replacing light bulbs or sharpening my eight hundred charcoal pencils, or I'm in my all-time best idea place—the shower!

Fairy Godmother. Age 6. Pencil and crayon on construction paper, 11¼ x 8¼".

"Draw a lot and never worry about staying inside the lines!"
—*Elise Primavera*

What is a normal day like for you?

I wake up around 7 to 7:30. I take a shower (get some ideas!) and then eat breakfast and read something. Reading seems to put me in the right frame of mind to begin work. By 9:00 I like to be at my drawing board. It's a big mistake for me to go outside my studio in the morning because once I'm out I never seem to be able to go back in!

I work best in the morning, which is why I try not to schedule meetings until after 2 P.M. By midmorning I have to resist the urge to call someone (usually I can't resist). By 12:00 my work area is such a mess I can no longer find anything, so I clean it up. I eat lunch, and then I can no longer resist chatting with someone. After lunch, I get back to work. Around 2:30 I'll go downstairs and check the mail, then get back to work. By 4:30 I've had it. I clean up in preparation for the next day.

By 5:30 I'm off to the gym where I work out or else I head outside for a run. Running (another place where I get my ideas!) has been a big part of my life ever since I stopped riding. It puts me in a really good mood after sitting all day. On the way home I pick up some dinner. Then I eat dinner, do some reading or watch TV, and go to bed around 11:00.

Where do you work?

I've always worked in a studio out of my home. I know being home all the time drives a lot of artists nuts, but it works well for me. I really like the idea of rolling out of bed in the morning and being in my studio without having to deal with the outside world in between

Do you have any children? Any pets?

No, which is strange since I like children and I like pets. Hmmmm, I'll need to think about this a bit further. . . . Maybe I need to get out of my house a little more?

What do you enjoy drawing the most?

I like to draw animals and people a lot. Also mountains and snow. I like to do night scenes, too. I like to do drawings with some humor in them, but I also enjoy doing scary, creepy stuff.

Do you ever put people you know in your pictures?

I used to use my camera a lot. I'd use my family and friends as models and have pictures of them to refer to when I made my illustrations. The grandmother character in *Grandma's House* and *Grandma's Promise* was a friend who owned the farm where I kept my horse, and the little girl character lived down the road from her.

But over the years I have phased out the use of photographs, mainly because I'm such a terrible photographer. I belong in the shoot-a-roll-of-film-with-my-finger-over-the-lens category. Now I try to rely on my memory to draw something or someone. Even without photos I still see my family and friends and even myself in my characters.

What do you use to make your pictures?

I've used a little bit of everything. When I first started I worked with pen and ink, pencil, and watercolor. Lately I've been working with pastels and acrylic. Pastels give my work a spontaneous quality and I can get richer and brighter colors.

I do all my preliminary sketches in charcoal on charcoal paper as well as on tracing paper. I start a piece by mixing gesso, an acrylic white paint, with pumice stone, which is a very grainy ground-up stone. I use that mixture to do an underpainting, covering my paper with it; if I don't, the pastels I use next will just dust off. The grainy paint gives the surface of my paper some "tooth," some texture for the pastels to hold onto. And if I make a mistake, it's easy to fix—the pastel smudges right out or I can put gesso over it.

How did you get to do your first book?

I tricked them—those pesky publishers! I drew a bunch of pictures that looked like I actually knew how to make a book. To give these pictures a professional appearance I then bought and placed them in a fancy leather holder called a portfolio.

Then, I left the portfolio in the lobbies of publishing companies all over New York City. Supposedly editors and art directors were going to look at my pictures while I was not there. I guess that was so I couldn't see them rolling on the floor with laughter. But I managed to fool someone because eventually I was asked to illustrate my first book!

Raising Dragons by Jerdine Nolen. 1998. Pastel, 15 x 20".
Published by Harcourt Brace.

Anna M. Rich

BIRTHDAY: July 2, 1956
Anna Rich

MY STORY

I am a native New Yorker. I grew up in the Bronx. I lived with my mom, dad, and sister in a big apartment house, which was an excellent situation for Halloween trick-or-treating because we canvassed the building a couple of times and didn't have to wear coats over our costumes. I was probably born an artist. I found a baby book my mom kept when I was little and under "Baby's First Words" my mom wrote, "Anna knows all her colors."

In kindergarten I recall staring at the easel set up in a corner, neat paint in cups, brushes, and a large pad of pristine paper clipped to it. Turns at the easel were taken alphabetically (you will recall my name begins with R) and Mrs. Ackerman didn't get around to easel painting it seemed for weeks, till I was almost frantic from waiting. I don't think I made any great art on that easel, since I would not have been as familiar with poster paint as with crayons, but I remember that wanting to be at that easel drowned out almost everything else that went on in kindergarten. This set the pattern for a lot of my elementary-school career. I would almost always have preferred drawing to just about anything with one important exception. I liked to read.

My mom kept us in crayons. One Christmas she found a box of 112 crayons, almost all different colors (or was it only 72?), with duplicates of the ones that got used up fast, like black and white. They were laid out flat in their box and came with a sharpener. To this day the aroma from a fresh box of crayons makes me calm and happy. In grade school I bought composition books so I could write and illustrate my own stories. I also filched scrap paper from my teacher for this purpose.

My stories were heavily influenced by the "girl stories" I got from the library (card member since 1964) and from watching *Days of Our Lives* with my grandfather after school. The stories were torrid, but nevertheless the text was limited to only so much space before an illustration had to be done.

From our bathroom window I discussed plot twists with my next-door best friend, Karen Felton, who was looking out her living room window and at work on her own story. I think our main characters were named Betsy, as were all the girls in the girl stories at the time. We didn't know anyone named Betsy in real life. Betsy was synonymous with "girl in a story" to us. We were also into paper dolls for a while and when Betsy (!) McCall's head got bent back so many times it fell off, we made our own paper dolls and then drew pages and pages of out-fits for them.

I did my first oil painting when I was about ten. My mom and dad knew I was an artist so I got an occasional art gift, like a paint-by-number set. I used paint that was left over from one of those kits and painted on a scrap of wood I picked up when our house was being built. We moved to Long Island where I live now. If you look closely at the piece, you'll see I did a preparatory sketch in yellow pencil. Nearly all of my work was done on manila paper, which is like newsprint or typing paper. This big piece of lumber is the only reason this early work has survived. I knew about watercol-ors and how to mix them some-what, but I had only a few colors and I didn't mix them the way I do now.

Girl with Bowl of Flowers.
Age 10.
Oil paint on wood,
7¼ x 13½ x 1½".

"If you like to do this kind of thing, do it, because it can't hurt you and it probably helps your brain develop."
—*Anna Rich*

Where do you get your ideas?
With a children's book I have to get my ideas from the text. Sometimes I get an idea from something I'll see, a blurry picture in a newspaper or a tiny picture in a magazine. In this instance, whatever I can see is too unclear for me to make out exactly what it is, but in that moment I get an idea for a picture. When I look at the thing more closely, it's not what I thought I saw and my idea will be completely different. Ideas also just pop into my head and I note them in a little sketch book so I don't forget.

What is a normal day like for you?

I wake up slowly. I don't use an alarm clock. I get a shower and a nice breakfast because I will fall back asleep if I don't have something to eat. I go to the studio and, depending on what kind of work I have to do, painting, drawing, or Everything Else, I either jump right on it, ease in slowly, or avoid it as long as possible, in that order. When I'm painting I often get so involved I have to make an effort to remember to drink enough water or change position. If the phone rings, I might pick it up but my mind may be too far away for me to make sense when I talk. I can get into drawing like that, too, but since I'm figuring out how things will look, it is more like work. I have to toss out and start again frequently and my eyes and hands get tired. I'm sure no one thinks of drawing and painting as being physically taxing, but they are.

I work until I get hungry. In the winter I know it's time for lunch (and dinner for that matter) because my nose and fingers get cold. Sometimes I work after dinner, especially if there's nothing I like on TV. I go to bed when I'm sleepy and usually read something from the great pile of books by my bed. When I'm having a rough time with my work I read fiction. When work is going okay I read everything else.

Where do you work?

I work in the studio on the ground level of my house. My desk is covered with paper, in fact paper is everywhere. I have a squirrel-proof bird feeder outside my window. I watch purple finches, blue jays, cardinals, juncos, and, of course, woodpeckers and house sparrows as they visit the feeder.

Dinah, queen of the universe.

Do you have any children? Any pets?

I have a cat, Dinah, a Brooklyn native.

What do you enjoy drawing the most?

I like to draw people. But I like to look at a painting longer when there are no people in it. Why? Because I can project myself into the picture. So, I look forward to including landscapes and environments in my paintings.

Do you ever put people you know in your pictures?

Yes, but not as often as I do dogs I have known. My nephew-dog Bart has been in four books; my husband Harry has found himself in two. I've put my dad, my nephew, Gilbert, and my friends (including other illustrators) in my paintings. I usually just think of them as I'm drawing. I don't make them pose or anything.

What do you use to make your pictures?

I make a pencil sketch, then trace it onto canvas and then use oil paint. Although my sketches are done in black, I get an idea from them of what my color choices will be for the final illustration.

How did you get to do your first book?

Well, it was one of those days when the work I had to do came under the aforementioned heading: Everything Else. All of a sudden, the phone rang!

It seems that a promotional piece showing one of my illustrations was passed along to an editor who liked my work. When you are a freelancer like I am, working for yourself, you have to send pictures to people at magazines and newspapers and publishers to show them your artwork. Even though I had forgotten about it and had moved since the card was printed, the editor tracked me down and asked me to illustrate *Joshua's Masai Mask.*

Annie's Gifts by Angela Shelf Medearis. 1994. Oil, 12½ x 10¹⁄₁₆".
Published by Just Us Books.

PETER SÍS

BIRTHDAY: May 11, 1949
Peter Sís

MY STORY

I was born in Brno and grew up in Prague, Czechoslovakia (now the Czech Republic). I have to credit my parents with giving me pencils and paper at a very early age, which was also the only way to keep the walls of our house clean. I remember illustrating stories my father told from Tibet, Borneo, Greece, and other places he had visited. I was always trying to imagine what the world looks like. I remember one night in my early teens when I drew with so much passion that I did not notice the night had gone and the sun was coming up.

There were some sweet surprises along the way. I illustrated posters for the movie *Amadeus* and for the New York subway, created designs for the Joffrey Ballet, and did a mural in the Baltimore/Washington International Airport. I lived through my book tours. I painted an Easter egg for the White House. I have a box of medals and awards, including a Caldecott Honor, and have an American passport. All these accomplishments seem miraculous, but the true miracle happened when my children Madeleine and Matej were born. With them my world has changed, my priorities have changed. My work is changing with them. They do not care about awards—they want to discover the world. And I want to try to help them.

I didn't grow up in this country, didn't eat pizza until I was about fifteen, and find peanut butter and jelly repulsive. I am learning to live with American culture and am lucky that I have an American wife who is both smart and pretty

(I mean patient). I am still finding out about the culture here. I was told that I should read have to my children while they were still in my wife's belly. As a freelancer dependent on happy clients I somehow missed doing that. I was told I should have read to my kids first thing in the morning, but they get up before 6 A.M. It is dark then and I am not good at that hour. I wait for *Sesame Street* or even for *Barney*. I know television is bad. I see the "lighthouse-like" expressions on my children's faces while they automatically suck on their bottles. I hate hearing those songs and alphabets over and over again. But maybe I'll get another fifteen minutes of sleep by allowing them to watch television so early in the morning. Luckily I have a wife who is both intelligent and educated, so she makes up for my indulgences.

The worst thing is when I cannot read to my kids because I have to go somewhere else to read to other people's kids from books I have written for my own kids. This travel is called promotion. Luckily I have a wife who is both American and tough. Even so, I may not go out and promote anymore.

I do not think life in America is all that bad. As a child I was brought up in more of an oral than a reading tradition. Some stories I was told were very, very scary, such as ones about the First World War or about children punished by torture for misbehaving. Later I read and believed Russian propaganda at school. I read Alexandre Dumas under my blanket. Maybe that is why I believe a little adversity doesn't hurt—and if I am wrong, I have a wife who . . .

Despite all I have just said, I have to say that Matej now regularly brings a book "to read" (about trucks). Madeleine completely shocked me the other day when she started to read me Wanda Gág's *Millions of Cats*. I was speechless, I was impressed. My wife had to explain to me that she had memorized everything. Actually, she can read most of the letters of the alphabet and count in Spanish, and knows our phone number—*what a country!*

Where do you get your ideas from?

I get ideas mostly from my past, from my childhood, from television or from newspapers, and now, recently, from my kids.

What is a normal day like for you?

Every day is basically the same. I take Madeleine to school at 8:30 A.M. I'm in the studio at 9:30 A.M. and I work until 4 or 4:30 P.M. Then I cook dinner so the kids can eat at 6:00. When they go to bed at 9:00, I am through for the day.

Where do you work?

I used to work at home but then the kids started to eat the paints. I was afraid they would get poisoned, so now my studio is five blocks away from home in a small studio apartment. I needed to have a kitchen because I like to dry my pictures in front of an oven.

Do you have any children? Any pets?

My daughter Madeleine is five years old. She loves ballerinas. My son Matej is three. He *is* a fire truck. When I read about ballerinas I do not know how to pronounce "curtsies" or "jeté." When I read about fire trucks I get confused between hook-and-ladder, pumpers, or lift-your-hose pumper truckers. The kids want a dog but I don't think we will have one in the city.

What do you enjoy drawing the most?

Water, because I'm from a landlocked country. We had no oceans where I grew up, no sea. We were surrounded by mountains, so I think water was always desirable for me.

Do you ever put people you know in your pictures?

I never did until I did a book about my childhood. I put my parents, my sister, and my brother in it. Since Madeleine, I think I put my kids in everything now.

What do you use to make your pictures?

Paper, ink, pen, and watercolors. Since 1992, I've been using golden frames. I use acrylic paint with gold pigment in it to create a sort of raised wall around the picture. It holds the watercolor in and also creates a nice effect.

Untitled. Age 8. Pen and ink, 8¼ x 5¼".

"Everyone starts somewhere. Even if the work is not perfect, everyone
has something to say, some story to tell. Just keep on trying."
—*Peter Sís*

How did you get to do your first book?

I always loved books. There was no television where I grew up. Books were the
window to the world. I would touch them, read them, illustrate them. I wanted
to be an artist. I remember my father's warning that an artist's life can get lonely
sometimes. Only much later did I realize that he was right. I went to art
schools, created paintings, posters, lithographs, costumes, and films. Animation
was my ticket to the world. I found work in Switzerland, England, and finally
Hollywood. However, things in Hollywood did not go exactly my way, and I
refused to paint backgrounds for the Smurfs series. What to do?

In the old country, I had gotten the Brothers Grimm's *Hansel and Gretel* to
illustrate in 1975. It was much easier to do books in that society, because there
was just one publishing house for children's books. It was a small place, so
everybody knew everybody. I had something of a reputation at art school and so
I kept bugging the publishers until they gave me a job.

I'd written to Maurice Sendak, who kindly introduced me to children's book
publishing in this country. It took some time, but many editorial illustrations
later, many illustrations for books of other authors later, and with eleven of my
own books now published, I am fine.

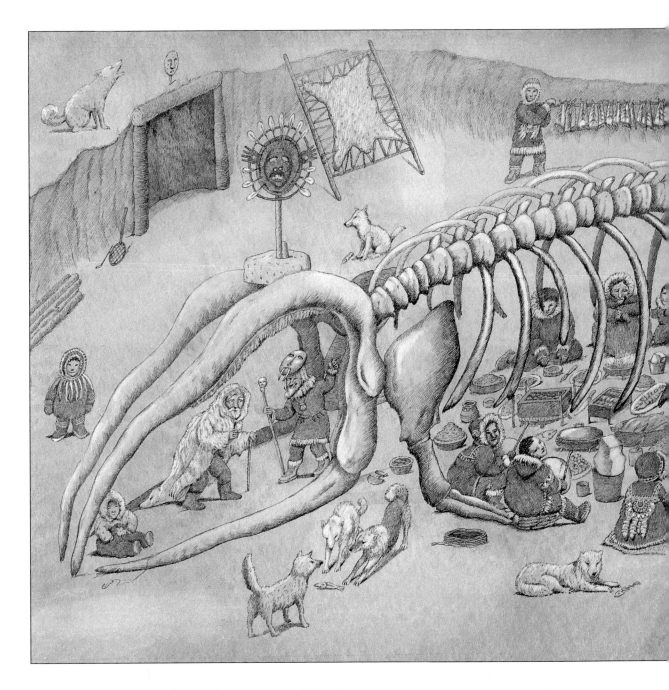

A Small, Tall Tale from the Far, Far North. 1993. Pen and ink and watercolor. 12½ x 10¹⁄₁₆". Published by Knopf.

Paul O. Zelinsky signature

BIRTHDAY: February 14, 1953
Paul O. Zelinsky

MY STORY

I was born quite young, at about age zero. A couple of years later I reached the age of two, at which time my family decided to move from an apartment near Chicago to a house in Kyoto, Japan. Our house was one of the only ones in Kyoto that didn't have walls made of paper. I wonder whether living in a city with paper for walls pushed me in the direction of drawing. I'm sure that living in a country where beautiful things are so deeply appreciated had something to do with it, although I was already a kid who liked to draw. (What two-year-old isn't?) At eighteen months I had produced my first recognizable drawing: a scribbly circle with two jabs for eyes and a crosswise slash for a mouth. "Baby!" I explained to my mother. "Boy!"

While living in Japan, I fell madly in love with the geisha. These mysterious ladies, who wore the most elegant silk robes and the most elaborately styled hair, swept me off my feet, and I tried to draw them.

After a year my father finished his studies in Japan and we moved back to America, to an apartment that looked out on a construction site. I drew tractors and steam shovels being driven by geisha. My parents observed that I was a bit mixed up. But I was getting better at drawing because I never stopped doing it. In nursery school, whenever we drew, my drawing would gather a little crowd of other four-year-olds. Secretly I loved the attention, but I told my sister that these crowds annoyed me, and I was going to put an end to them. My plan was to make an extremely bad drawing. The next time we had art in school I drew a big rectangle with two stabs for eyes and a slash for a mouth. In spite of my best effort, everyone gathered around and admired how interesting my work was. And that is how modern art was invented (just kidding). But perhaps it meant that I was destined to be an artist.

My mother was, and is, an artist, a medical illustrator. She made pictures of the insides of people for doctors who needed such things. I liked to look at her books of anatomy and draw the skeletons in them.

I grew a little older, and was skinny and nearsighted and hopeless in all sports. (And I still am. But I have very strong finger and thumb muscles that never get tired.) At home, when I wasn't reading, I was drawing or painting on the back of my father's used exam papers. It was always fun trying new things, new materials, new techniques. One particular pad of thick, creamy paper seemed to inspire the most unexpected moves. I remember making a watercolor landscape on it and then adding little airplanes and clouds made of clay. (Unfortunately, the clay kept falling off when it dried.) The feeling of surprise that comes when you make something you didn't expect—and you like it—is something wonderful. I still hope for that feeling when I work, and wish it came around more often.

The books I illustrate are very different from one another, and I love that fact. It makes me try different things, new techniques, unfamiliar styles. Sometimes I disappoint myself. Sometimes I surprise myself. When I do, it keeps me feeling young; a nice feeling, now that I'm not as young as I was when I was young.

"The more you draw, the more you learn about the visible world around you."
—*Paul Zelinsky*

Geisha.
Age 3 years and 10 months.
Pencil, 5½ x 8½ ".

Where do you get your ideas?

I get a real idea, a good idea about how to make something out of nothing, only once every few years, if that. And I don't know where it comes from; I just notice it hanging around, like a dog without an owner. But for ideas about how to illustrate something already written—I find the answers in the writing. I just read very carefully and realistically, and try to match with my pictures what is already there in the words.

What is a normal day like for you?

My average day is ruled by my family's schedule. My wife is a teacher and my daughters go to school, so I'm up in the morning, get to my studio by 8:45, and start my day. It might be a day to do research for a project, so I might go to the library when it opens, or it might be a day to do sketches or plan out a book, or I might be at the stage of making finished drawings or paintings.

I try to get home by 5:30 or so, unless I'm behind on a deadline. Then I might go back to work in the evening after supper with my family. I have always liked the night, and I have been known to go on working past my bedtime.

Where do you work?

My studio is a one-room apartment a short walk, or an even shorter bicycle ride, from the apartment where my family lives.

Do you have any children? Any pets?

I have two daughters, born in 1984 and 1988. Anna's due date was the same as my delivery date for *Hansel and Gretel,* and Rachel came out at about the same time as *The Random House Book of Humor for Children.*

Our Siamese cat is named Skimbleshanks, Skimby for short.

What do you enjoy drawing the most?

I enjoy doodling, and when I am doodling I never know what I will draw next. What's already there decides what comes next. I like to draw trees from my imagination, but I have a hard time drawing them from life. Monsters are always pleasant, too.

Do you ever put people you know in your pictures?

The models for the characters in my books are rarely people I know. But often I need to get a slightly different angle on a pose, or some other variation when the model isn't around, so my books are full of elbows, hands, or feet of various unidentified friends and relatives. But both of my daughters are characters in *The Wheels on the Bus.* And two-year-old Anna was the train-bearer for the queen's wedding dress in *Rumpelstiltskin.*

What do you use to make your pictures?

I like to draw or paint with all sorts of materials. When things aren't going well, what often can pull me back to inspiration is some new color of paint or an unfamiliar paper. I've illustrated books with pastels, with watercolor, with pen and ink, with colored pencils and with gray pencils, with oil paints, with gouache or opaque watercolors. I've worked on all sorts of paper, and *Swamp Angel* was painted in oils on super-thin wood, but I make sure that everything I do for a book is the right size and flexibility to fit around the drum of a scanner. Scanning on a drum scanner, at least at this time of the century, makes possible the finest reproduction when a piece of art gets printed.

How did you get to do your first book?

When I was in college, I took a course on the history and making of picture books. A writer in the class teamed up with me on projects for a number of picture books. We sent copies of our planned books to many publishers, and one of them accepted one of our stories. It would have been my first book, if the publisher had not been immediately bought by another, bigger publisher, and dissolved.

But that was how I first made myself known to publishers. When I eventually decided to move to New York and try for real to become an illustrator, I showed my drawings to all the same publishers again, and one of them happened to need an illustrator for a novel by Avi. It was called *Emily Upham's Revenge, or How Deadwood Dick Saved the Banker's Niece, A Massachusetts Adventure.* It was not a large book; the challenge was to get all that title onto the front of it and leave room for any picture at all. How lucky that Avi has such a short name!

Rapunzel.
1997. Oil, 8¼ x 11¼".
Published by Dutton Children's Books.

SECRET TECHNIQUES ••••••••••••••••••••

Peter Catalanotto

If you want to make something look as if it's moving in your drawing, you can rub with your eraser. Don't rub too hard or you'll just erase your picture!

Color in parts of your picture.   Smear with your eraser.

Lisa Desimini

I do a pencil drawing, then put white acrylic all over the board except where the pencil line is. Then I begin to glaze with oil paints, going from light to dark. I might use yellow ochre, sap green, burnt sienna, alizarin crimson, then thalo blue. I glaze with a squirt of paint and a blob of Liquin, then smear it everywhere. Since there was no white acrylic where the pencil line was, a darker stain is left that gives me a loose impression of my drawing. I'm ready to paint, having all of those beautiful colors already in place.

Jane Dyer

To help me draw better, whether it is animals, cars, clothing, houses, or anything, I always gather pictures of my subject. I can't draw a pig or a horse or a cow very well without references. But the trick is to then combine research with imagination to make each thing uniquely my own. For example, when drawing animals, dressing them helps—and a few flowing ribbons often provide just the right finishing touch!

Kevin Hawkes

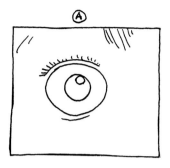

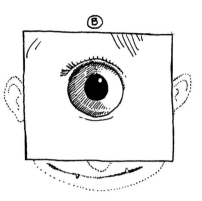

When drawing an eye, start with three circles: A large one for the eyeball, a medium one for the pupil, and a tiny one for the "highlight."

Then when you shade the eye in, make the middle circle really dark and leave the "highlight" circle completely white. This makes the eye look shiny and real.

G. Brian Karas

Try this: Cut out an interesting magazine or newspaper picture. Glue it on a stiff piece of paper. Let the glue dry, then paint and draw over it so that some of the picture underneath shows through. Then you have two pictures in one.

Betsy Lewin

One of the great things about working on tracing paper is that you can keep parts of a drawing that you like and change the parts you're not satisfied with. Or you can change your mind about a gesture or an expression and replace it with another. For instance, I liked the gesture of the horse below, but I couldn't decide whether he should be eating grass or looking at the reader. I put tracing paper over the horse and drew the head in both positions and chose one. Then I cut it out and taped it in place with bits of Magic Tape. In the final drawing no one can tell how many stages it went through to get there.

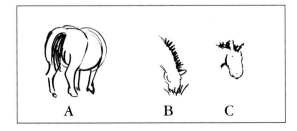

A   B   C

A + B

A + C

Ted Lewin

Here's how to get your value patterns and form right: Squint at your subject, then squint at your drawing. Squinting simplifies values and form.

Keiko Narahashi

I think artists are very conscious of shadows. Shadows have a lot of information in them: where an object is located, which direction the light is coming from. Without shadows things look as if they're floating in some indefinite space.

A ball. Some-where in outer space maybe.

A ball on the ground.

A ball bouncing.

A ball bouncing off the wall.

A ball hitting the ceiling.

Elise Primavera

When I'm figuring out a drawing, it helps if I look at the image reversed. Hold your drawing in front of a mirror to reverse the image. Or try this. You will need:

- tracing paper
- charcoal 6B pencil
- chamois cloth (ask the salesperson in an art store)

1. Do a quick drawing on tracing paper.

2. Now turn it over. Wow! I see what's wrong when I look at it now.

3. Fix the drawing so that even the back-ward view looks correct.

4. Turn it over, then wipe the old drawing off the front with the chamois cloth.

5. Keep working back and forth until it looks right from both the front *and* back.

WOW! MUCH BETTER!

Anna Rich

I didn't learn this technique until I got to art school. My teacher, Mahler Ryder, insisted we draw a border inside the edges of a sheet of paper before drawing. This makes it easier to think about composition and makes your drawing strong.

the paper

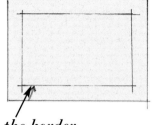
the border

a close-up within the border

Try to fill the space and not have things floating around. You can think of making things go "off the screen," close up or far away. Having that border will make it easy to frame your work on paper.

Paul O. Zelinsky

I don't think I'll ever get over a certain excitement at drawing one side of an object pale, and the other side dark, to create the effect of a light shining on the object from one side. The technical word for this effect is *chiaroscuro,* which is just Italian for "light-dark," but sounds so much more romantic. If I'm using color, I often like to make the dark shadow not blackish but a nice blue. Shadows are very blue in the outdoors, because the part where the yellowish sunlight isn't hitting an object is probably still exposed to the richly colored, but not very bright, blue light from the sky.

BOOKS BY THE ARTISTS ·•·•·•·•·•·•·•·•·•

All the artists were asked to name four or five favorite books that they've illustrated. If the artist didn't also write the book, the author's name is given, so you'll be able to find it in your library or bookstore.

Peter Catalanotto
Book. D.K. Ink, by George Ella Lyon. 1998.
Dylan's Day Out. Orchard Books, 1989.
Letter to the Lake by Susan Marie Swanson. DK Ink, 1998.
Mr. Mumble. Orchard Books, 1990.
Who Came Down That Road? by George-Ella Lyon. Orchard Books, 1992.

Raúl Colón
Buoy, at Home at Sea by Bruce Balan. Bantam, Doubleday, Dell, 1998.
Celebration! by Jane Resh Thomas. Disney Press, 1997.
My Mama Had a Dancing Heart by Libba Moore Gray. Orchard Books, 1996.
Tomas and the Library Lady by Pat Mora. Random House, 1997.
A Weave of Words by Robert D. San Souci. Orchard Books, 1998.

Lisa Desimini
Doodle Dandies: Poems at a Glance by J. Patrick Lewis. Simon & Schuster, 1998.
In a Circle Long Ago: A Treasury of Native Lore from North America. Knopf, 1995.
Moon Soup. Hyperion, 1993.
My House. Henry Holt, 1994.
Tulip Sees America by Cynthia Rylant. Scholastic, 1998.

Jane Dyer
*Animal Crackers: A Delectable Collection of Pictures, Poems, and Lullabies for the
    Very Young.* Little, Brown and Co., 1996.
Child of Faerie by Jane Yolen. Little, Brown and Co., 1997.
Piggins by Jane Yolen. Harcourt Brace, 1987.
Talking Like the Rain: A First Book of Poems edited by Dorothy M. Kennedy and
    selected by X. J. Kennedy. Little, Brown and Co., 1992.
Time for Bed by Mem Fox. Harcourt Brace, 1993.

Kevin Hawkes

By the Light of the Halloween Moon by Caroline Stutson. Lothrop, Lee & Shepard, 1993.

The Librarian Who Measured the Earth by Kathryn Lasky. Little, Brown and Co., 1994.

Marven of the Great North Woods by Kathryn Lasky. Harcourt Brace & Co., 1997.

Painting the Wind: A Story of Vincent van Gogh by Michelle Dionetti. Little, Brown and Co., 1996.

The Turnip by Walter De La Mare. David Godine Publisher, 1992.

G. Brian Karas

Home on the Bayou: A Cowboy's Story. Simon & Schuster, 1996.

I Know an Old Lady. Scholastic, 1995.

In the Hush of the Evening by Nancy Price Graffe. HarperCollins, 1998.

Saving Sweetness by Diane Stanley. Putnam, 1996.

The Windy Day Simon & Schuster, 1998.

Betsy Lewin

Booby Hatch. Clarion Books, 1995.

Chubbo's Pool. Clarion Books, 1996.

No Such Thing by Jackie French Koller. Boyds Mills Press, 1997.

What If the Shark Wears Tennis Shoes? by Winifred Morris. Atheneum, 1990.

Yo—Hungry Wolf?: A Nursery Rap by David Vozar. Dell, 1995.

Ted Lewin

Cowboy Country by Ann Herbert Scott. Clarion Books, 1993.

The Day of Ahmed's Secret by Florence Parry Heide and Judith Heide Gilland. Lothrop, Lee & Shepard, 1990.

Market! Lothrop, Lee & Shepard, 1996.

Peppe the Lamplighter by Elisa Bartone. Lothrop, Lee and Shepard, 1993.

Sacred River. Clarion Books, 1995.

Keiko Narahashi

A Is for Amos. Farrar, Straus and Giroux, 1999.

Is That Josie? McElderry Books, 1994.

The Magic Purse by Yoshiko Uchida. Margaret K. McElderry Books, 1993.

What's What? A Guessing Game by Mary Serfozo. Margaret K. McElderry Books, 1996.

Who Said Red? by Mary Serfozo. Margaret K. McElderry Books, 1988.

Elise Primavera

Christina Katerina and the Time She Quit the Family by Patricia Lee Gauch. Putnam, 1987.

Jack, Skinny Bones, and the Golden Pancakes by Mary-Claire Helldorfer. Viking Penguin, 1996.

Moe the Dog in Tropical Paradise. by Diane Stanley. Putnam, 1992.

Moonlight Kite by Helen Elizabeth Buckley. Lothrop, Lee & Shepard, 1997.

Plant Pet. Putnam, 1994.

Anna Rich

Cleveland Lee's Beale Street Band by Arthur Flowers. BridgeWater Books, 1996.

From My Window by Olive Thurman Wong. Silver Burdett Press, 1994.

Joshua's Masai Mask by Dakari Hru. Lee & Low Books, 1993.

Just Right Stew by Karen English. Boyds Mills Press, 1998.

Saturday at the New You by Barbara E. Barber. Lee & Low Books, 1994.

Peter Sís

Firetruck. Greenwillow, 1998.

Follow the Dream. Knopf, 1991.

Komodo! Greenwillow, 1993.

Starry Messenger: Galileo Galilei. Farrar, Straus and Giroux, 1996.

Three Golden Keys. Doubleday, 1994.

Paul Zelinsky

The Maid and the Mouse and the Odd-Shaped House. Dutton Children's Books, 1993.

Rumpelstiltskin. Dutton Children's Books, 1986.

The Story of Mrs. Lovewright and Purrless Her Cat by Lore Segal. Knopf, 1985.

Swamp Angel by Anne Isaacs. Dutton Children's Books, 1994.

The Wheels on the Bus: With Pictures that Move. Dutton Children's Books, 1990.

•••••••••• ACKNOWLEDGMENTS ••••••••••

Grateful acknowledgment is given to the artists who participated in this book and for permission to reproduce their photographs and samples of their childhood artwork. Our appreciation, too, to the following individuals and publishers.

Page 11.   Photo credit: Jo Maynard

Page 13.   Photo credit: Jo Maynard

Page 14–15.   From *The Painter,* written and illustrated by Peter Catalanotto. Illustrations copyright © 1995 by Peter Catalanotto. Reprinted by permission of Orchard Books.

Page 17.   Photo credit: Bernd Nobel

Page 21.   From *Always My Dad,* written by Sharon Dennis Wyeth. Copyright © 1995 by Raúl Colón. Reprinted by permission of Knopf.

Page 22.   Photo credit: Mr. and Mrs. Desimini

Page 23.   Photo credit: Matt Mahurin

Page 26–27.   From *Love Letters,* written by Arnold Adoff. Copyright © 1997 by Lisa Desimini. Reprinted by permission of The Blue Sky Press, an imprint of Scholastic Books, Inc.

Page 29.   Photo credit: Brooke and Cecily Dyer

Page 31.   Photo credit: Jane Dyer

Page 32.   From *Child of Faerie,* written by Jane Yolen. Copyright © 1997 by Jane Dyer. Reprinted by permission of Little, Brown and Co.

Page 35.   Photo credit: Jamie Hogan

Page 39.   From *My Little Sister Ate One Hare,* written by Bill Grossman. Copyright © 1996 by Kevin Hawkes. Reprinted by permission of Crown Books.

Page 41.   Photo credit: Sue Karas

Page 43.   Photo credit: Brian Karas

Page 44–45.   From *Sleepless Beauty,* written by Frances Minters. Copyright © 1996 by G. Brian Karas. Reprinted by permission of Viking Books.

Page 47.   Photo credit: Ted Lewin

Page 49.   Photo credit: Ted Lewin

Page 50–51.   From *What's the Matter, Habibi?* Copyright © 1997 by Betsy Lewin. Used by permission of Clarion Books.

Page 53.   Photo credit: Betsy Lewin

Page 55.   Photo credit: Ted Lewin

Page 56–57.   From *Fair.* Copyright © 1996 by Ted Lewin. Reprinted by permission of Viking Books.

Page 58.   Photo credit: Toshio Narahashi

Page 59.   Photo credit: Peter Belamarich

Page 62–63.   From *I Have a Friend.* Copyright © 1987 by Keiko Narahashi. Used by permission of McElderry Books.

Page 65.   Photo credit: Francis McCall

Page 69.   From *Raising Dragons,* written by Jerdine Nolen. Copyright © 1998 by Elise Primavera. Used by permission of Harcourt Brace.